Poems From A Pure Heart

David Murdoch

BookLeaf Publishing

Presentation by *BookLeaf Publishing*

Web: www.bookleafpub.com

E-mail: info@bookleafpub.com

ISBN: 9789357445429

First edition 2021

DEDICATION

I would like to dedicate this new poetry book to the FOUR people for whom I have the greatest respect and love. Each one of them helped me create the set of values by which I live my life now.

My late parents Ernie and Mollie,

My little big sister Sharon, and most importantly my dearest companion, my beautiful darling wife Pauline.

ACKNOWLEDGEMENT

I would like to acknowledge the hard work of the people at Bookleaf Publishing who have printed and published this poetry collection for me. I could not have done it without you. Thank-you, one and all.

I would like to acknowledge also the support of my friends in the Wellness Recovery Network [WRN] in the South Eastern Trust here in Northern Ireland who have encouraged me to keep writing my poetry and to get it printed, in order for it to be read and enjoyed by a wider audience of people. WRN is a truly wonderful unique support group helping our communities, and I have made so many genuine friends through it.

I desire also to acknowledge our many global friends who take the time to engage with me online, mainly through my Facebook account. Your support has been invaluable. I look forward to the news, jokes, experiences, and the interchange of encouragement between us. Thanks a million folks, you know who you are!

And finally I acknowledge the support of my loving wife Pauline who has helped me through my various health crises and makes everything worthwhile. I couldn't have done any of this without your assistance. I love you so much, now and forever.

PREFACE

Poetry, in my opinion, should engage the senses. It should help us create images in our minds as we read the words aloud.

I have written poetry for my own pleasure for several years. I like writing free verse but overall I prefer meter or rhyme. In recent years I got into journaling on a daily basis and I now try to write poetry every day even if it is only a few lines.

In my opinion poetry connects us to our emotions and it definitely allows me to express my deepest feelings or translate the personal stories of some of our friends.

While I might have employed various presentation styles throughout this book, each poem within these covers has been written from the heart. It is my sincere wish that you will find some lines inside that will lift your spirits, touch your soul, and resonate with your heart as well.

David Murdoch.
davidmpoet@gmail.com

A New Youth Anthem: "We're Going To Change The World!"

We're going to change the world we are
We're going to change the world!
We're taking plastic from the seas
And going to plant a billion trees
Find out how to make the Arctic refreeze
Because we're going to change the world.

We're going to change the world we are
We're going to change the world!
We want an end to fossil fuel cars
We'll stop them sending rockets to Mars
And promise to landscape Mother Earth's scars
Because we're going to change the world.

We're going to change the world we are
We're going to change the world!
Everyone is going to get equal pay
The bankers no longer will get their way
Ordinary people will have the final say
Because we're going to change the world.

We're going to change the world we are
We're going to change the world!
We'll ban the bomb and get world peace
Live sustainably beside clean seas
And get the polluters to all cease
Because we're going to change the world.
Yes we are!
We're going to change the world.

To My Wife.

You are the brightest star in my galaxy
The shining moon of my evening sky
You are the sunlight upon the moving waters
You are my reason why.

You are the loveliest deep red rose
In the garden of my heart you lie
You are the strongest beat of my beating heart
You are my reason why.

You are the icing on the sweetest cake
In a shop of gateaux and pie
You are my perfect partner
You are my reason why.

You are the most perfect note
In that symphony played on high
You are the person I love most deeply
You are my reason why.

You are the young girl I married
True soul mates are you and I
In sickness, health and forever.
You are my reason why.

Where Did I Go To?

Whatever happened to the long hot days of August
That we enjoyed in our childhood years?
As we played in the long meadow grass
And wandered through the woods and hills
Splashing in the open brook
And drinking water from a gurgling spring
Oblivious to the dangers or the mind of predators
Collecting scars on our elbows and our knees like trophies
Faces streaked red from berries picked in the wild
Knowledge learned from experience or by daring one another
Into climbing trees or rolling down the slopes
The air ringing with our laughter and our yells
The whoops and hollers of innocent play
Until real hunger drove us homeward
Swinging a stick around our head
Having done battle with a dragon and come off victorious
Or single handedly fought against an enemy horde
Without a scratch except where the brambles ripped our summer shorts!
Whatever happened to those days of freedom?
I guess, more's the pity, we grew up
And trapped that carefree child deep inside.

On Seeing The Heavens Laid Out Upon The Green.

I wrote this poem as my homage to the great Irish poet William Butler Yeats.

~~~~~~~~~~~~

"On Seeing The Heavens Laid Out Upon The Green."

When stars of heaven fall to earth,
They lie scattered on the greenest turf,
And as we walk along this milky way
Starlight blooms light up our day,
As galaxy petals catch the dew
Scented roses our senses do renew.
We lightly tread upon a lawn of stars
And dream about more pleasant hours
Let us meander while we may
For who of us dare ever say,
"I know tomorrow guaranteed for sure!"
When all we have is this single moment pure.
Friends, walk with pleasure upon this pasture green
Enjoy the day, the pleasures seen,
~~~~~~~~~~~~

And if a falling star your eye does see,
Pray, make your wish, then wander free.

On The Loss Of A Loved One.

Can you hear me my lover?
I thought I heard you calling
As I walked out among the trees
Ah sure it is simply leaves rustling
Caught on a brief summer's breeze.

Can you hear me my lover?
I thought I heard you talking
As the house settled down for the night
That's only the old floorboards squeaking
It would give anybody a fright.

Can you hear me my lover?
I thought I caught you whispering
As I strolled on the riverbank walk
It is just the waterfowl in the rushes
That sound like the reeds filled with talk.

Can you hear me my lover?
I know that your voice has gone from this world
Since the sad afternoon that you died
For I cannot hear you my lover
No matter how long or much I have cried.

Can you hear me my lover?
I am sure that I heard you speaking
Today in the church when I knelt
Your words caressed me so softly
Tenderly in my heart were they felt.

It was the place where we were married
And I sensed you there in the quiet
I turned but there was no-one at all
Yet I heard you there my sweet lover
And I stand by awaiting your call.

Hold On To Your Precious Treasure.

There’s many a day when I become depressed
My gentle wife will me caress
She will not pressure or chastise me
And even knows when to let things be
Without her help in days of strife
I hate to contemplate where my life
Might have gone when dark thoughts were rife
Which is why I cherish my most precious wife.

If you have a partner who is kind
Who treats you well and doesn't mind
When you are happy or if you are sad
But helps push back the dark and bad
Then please whenever you are feeling better
Tell them how much you love and treasure
Everything they have done for you
For their expressions of love are true.

You and your partner will face many trials
There’s both good and bad times down the miles
But together with love you will get there
For that is what it means to share
It is easy to use the words "I love you"
When life is rosy and storms are few

It's when darkness comes and problems with them
That you'll know if you have found a gem.

If after all the debris has been swept away
You want to be with them, yes come what may
Then you can see how far you have travelled together
For such never-ending love survives no matter what the weather.

Alarming News.

When my alarm buzzed
I hit the snooze button
For an extra five minutes
In the comfort of my bed.
And 52 more children
Under the age of five
Died.

* According to the website www.theirworld.org at least 15,000 children under the age of five die each day across the globe.

Aftermath.

⚠ Trigger Warning. ⚠
⚠ This poem describes the loss of a baby and unresolved grief.⚠

Clodagh bakes bread and Roland squeezes squelchy clay
Both pairs of hands knead and pound
Daily in silence they avoid each other's glances
While bittersweet emotions take up lodging with regret.

She was almost carried to full term
They'd painted the smallest room in pastel shades
Disagreed laughingly over names to call her,
Until they were ready to welcome their Ciara home.

The ending though was unexpected despite a roomful of medical expertise
Shock! Tears, disbelief and especially grief
And neither one could face the emptiness they felt inside.

She hated those words "you lost your baby girl"
As if accidentally, after a picnic, they'd somehow misplaced her in the woods
She hated the way her body had failed her
Not to deliver, not to let her even see Ciara outside of her mind.

So Clodagh works silently in her modern kitchen
Angry, frustrated, humbled and afraid.

Whereas in his garden studio Roland screams, he shouts and swears
Manipulating lumps of potter's clay into shapes and abstract forms
His hands, channelling his grief, makes it bend to suit his will
He loves Clodagh dearly, much more than sculptured clay, he always will
But so much needs said that he yet cannot say.
In the meantime he is the creator of something new
Filled with passion from his skilful hands
But in the end his creation will remain a piece of lifeless stillborn clay.
If only - but no! That's unfair
Impossible to compare this lifeless modelling clay with motherhood.

She wipes the flour off her apron, and wipes away sudden tears from her eyes
That flow as swiftly as the river, her namesake, rising in distant Lough Coumduala
Up in the Comeragh range of mountains in Ireland's Waterford county, Clodagh.
She sniffs and her wrist wipes more tears away.

As to herself, she ponders how easy it is to create fresh bread,
To see how the yeast unseen to her eyes works its rise

Changing in form with oven's heat into a living life-giving thing
Yet (what is that awful phrase?)
Her 'bun in the oven' did not rise, there was no substance giving life to Ciara in the end
And with her death it was as if Clodagh's heart had also died.

Clodagh bakes bread while Roland kneads his clay
Both of them need each other
But not just yet, to resume the natural intimacy, because of their regret.
It doesn't stop well-meaning though thoughtless friends exclaim "you're both still young. You'll have another."
Perhaps.
But not Ciara, no not her.
And not while Clodagh bakes and Roland moulds his clay.

Time Travellers And Lovers Two.

On a cold snowy day in winter
Wrapped up against the sleet
We walked by that frozen river
And marched on two stout feet.
We stopped at the wooden bridge
Where watching the birds in the wood
We said that we'd be together
Through both bad times and the good.
Years have passed since that winter's day
Our limbs have grown weaker
It's easy to forget the good things
And only see life as bleaker.
But that's not the way we do it
That isn't for me and you
We shall always have our good times
Even should they number few.
We wrap up warm and safely
As we journey through life's weather
Keep holding hands, sharing love's dreams,
We succeed as a couple together.

War! Why? Who Decides?

A man takes a holiday in foreign parts. He is friendly and cheerful, and by the end of a week is chatting to the locals, sharing jokes and drinks, joining in the laughter at the local bar and restaurant. He already knows a few by name and they greet him as he arrives each night.

A month or so after he comes back home the politicians of his country have a falling out with those in foreign parts. As a patriotic citizen the man enlists and is given a blue uniform. He is told that anyone in a uniform of red needs to be taken out, shot dead.

The soldiers dressed in red are told that if they see a man in blue, to run him through!
Battles are fought, bodies are piled high. Sentries are killed from behind, a broken neck or a slit across the throat. Men lose limbs and some lose their minds.

One day a leading general blows his whistle and waving his arms cries to his men to STOP because the war is over....
Handing in their guns they learn that someone has brokered a peace deal between the two sides and all the fighting is over.

The man, fortunately enough unscarred and more or less unscathed, goes back to his old life and job. In time he falls in love, begins a family. And after a few years he treats his family to a foreign holiday.

They are friendly and cheerful, and by the end of a week are chatting to the locals, sharing jokes, games and drinks, joining in the laughter at the local bar and restaurant.

Some remember him from many years ago as a younger man. He surprises himself that he still knows a few by name and they greet him as he arrives each night. He shows them snapshots of his family and his home, they do the same.

No one mentions that awful war of course - it's all in the past.
His family enjoy their holiday and his daughter has gotten a nice new penpal to keep in touch with for years to come.

What personality disorder changed in this man that between his two visits of friendliness he was willing to butcher anyone from that foreign country?
None.
He only did those awful things because two sets of politicians in far off rooms couldn't reach a diplomatic settlement, and someone declared a war.

For him, he says, it was nothing personal. Yet the waiter who slapped him on the back just last week and laughed at his jokes would have slit his throat during the war. And he would have killed the laughing barmaid's husband had he met him on the battlefield dressed in red.

Such is the stupidity of war.

To kill those who we do not know in person, just because someone else whom we have never met says that we must.
Who really is the enemy here?
Perhaps, (as my paternal grandfather used to say after he and all his brothers fought in World War 1), if those who decide to take a country into war would instead climb into the boxing ring and slug it out with their counterparts on the opposite side, the chances are that it would STOP at the first busted nose or broken tooth.

We are all human beings. We have the same emotions. We protect our friends. How do we not know that we might not equally love the same things as the people over there? Especially if we met them on holiday or in happier times?

Such is the futility of war.

Stop The Global Abuse Of Women Now.

Watching the news in recent weeks left me feeling so angry, between the plight of those women fleeing conflict in North Africa and Afghanistan, human trafficking in Europe, pre-teen brides in certain countries, or domestic violence and abuse here in the UK. All females who need help NOW, not just promises of one day in the future. Our society needs to do more to stop the global abuse of women.

~~~~~~~~~~~

I hurt because of how you lied to me
I hurt because of what you denied to me
I hurt because of what you said to friends
I hurt because you demand your own ends
I hurt because you beat me black
I hurt because of how you took me back
I hurt because of the money you stole
I hurt because I was burnt with coal
I hurt because I could tell no-one
I hurt as you laughed and said it's fun
I hurt because you stripped me bare
I hurt because of what you made me share
I hurt because I have the welts
I hurt where you cut me with those belts
~~~~~~~~~~~

I hurt because you took away my child
I hurt because you were cruel and wild
I hurt because of your drunken rages
I hurt because you stole all my wages
I hurt because you made me your slave
I'll hurt until I reach my grave
What gives you the right to treat me so?
How dare you say I am old or slow
I hurt because you took away my food
I hurt because you knew you could
I hurt because you say you're the Man
I hurt just because you think you can
I hurt in every nation and each land
I hurt because you use a forceful hand
I hurt because you have the power
I hurt because you make me cower
I hurt because you bound me in ropes
I hurt because you destroyed all my hopes
I hurt where you made me become your wife
I hurt because it's still not my life
I hurt when you branded my poor skin
I hurt when you forced yourself deep within
I hurt because you shaved my bruised head
I hurt where I am and wherever I fled
I hurt because I hurt, and I hurt and hurt
And yet you continue to treat me as dirt
I hurt
I hurt
I hurt
I HURT.

My Life Is A Poem.

I once cried out, "I have no purpose anymore, I have no job, no idea of who I am since my three strokes and my deep depression."

Life said in return "Write, for your words are your gift. You can raise others up with you and together touch the stars."

My life is a Poem, and a journey of faith. A path of my own choosing and times of being lost.

Sometimes the words matter and resonate with the beat of my heart.
Sometimes it is the pauses, the silence between the words, which carry my thoughts.
And look, you are reading my words and in your mind's eye are seeing my story one step at a time; making a comparison to your own storyline.

Together we will rise! First to our knees, and pause in silent prayer.
Then to our feet and gulp down fresh air, lifting our head and looking up to the skies.
Standing there in the afternoon of our lives until twilight when we begin to see the farthest galaxies, and together we can touch the stars.

My life is a Poem. A unique journey back to power. Where what I once was is unimportant now, what I once did is gone, lost in the fog of my depression. But I have moved on. Each verse tells my story in simple ways. You have your own path yet can turn to mine to watch for familiar stepping stones to follow.

Together, we will touch the stars, and raise awareness of our journey to recovery. We will raise our hands and stretch out our fingers to the brightest sun a million light years or more away.
It makes us feel small and at the same time larger than life itself. We are all one on this journey of hope. We are the promise of a better tomorrow. We are recovering from where we once were. We are the words.

Because life is a Poem. And together we will touch the stars.

No-One Chooses To Become Mentally Ill.

About 3 years ago I was invited to read several pieces of my poetry at a mental health forum in Belfast. I wrote this piece for the event and concluded my poetry reading with it. Since then, it has become one of the most requested poems I am invited to read.

~~~~~~~~~~~

They say that your health is wealth
Well I know there's gold in my teeth and silver in my hair
But what about my mental health
What treasures are there, there?

Well there's a lifetime of my memories
And lived experience too
There's stamina and courage
Gained from what I have been through

There's endurance and a hidden strength
There's empathy and care
This is like a seam of solid gold
If my mental soul's laid bare
~~~~~~~~~~~

There are elements from a previous life
Before I took so ill
And then promises for a new one
Which brings a certain thrill

I need a mental detector
To scan across my mind
To identify the treasures or
The dross to be left behind

Because I firmly do believe
As we invest in our new life
We are focusing on recovery
And not just the previous strife

Don't let your critic deceive you
Ignore that nasty inside voice
Tell yourself your value
Yes sit up and rejoice

Say, "I am worth my weight in gold,"
"I'm priceless beyond compare"
"I've treasure in my self-esteem"
"Like a diamond, oh so rare."

So let me finish with these words
For myself and all who's here
You are precious, if not priceless
You are someone very dear.

We Are All In This Together.

I am a citizen of this planet earth
You could call me a Terran by right of birth
My family embodies every human man
Each woman and each child inside every land.
Skin colour does not matter nor our languages
Since we're joined by the drum beat of our heart
The same pulse of life that courses through our veins
And the fact that we never have to live apart.
You are my sister and my brother too
You are my daughter and my son
You are my father and my mother true
You are me and I am you since we are one.
I am a citizen of this planet earth
You laugh sometimes at my joyfulness
Whereas my heart breaks at your awful plight
Why can't we live together with peacefulness.
Surely you want food, clothes and shelter
Family members and the gift of love
The same reasons we all are living
On our one planet with the blue sky above.
Let us hold out our hands and open up
Our hearts to the possibility of it please
All souls together on this beautiful marbled earth
Let us at least try and make for peace.

Do Your Eyes Behold Him?

God visits our neighbourhood every day
And shows himself in way after way
We see his beauty in the trees
Admire his power when the breeze
Becomes a howling windy gale
Discover how from the little snail
To the flying majestic birds above
And every flower and garden shrub
Is evidence of his creative hand
All made out of common sand
We see his glory in the sun
Shining bright as day's begun
We reflect on this plus the rain
Which soaks the earth so again
Life springs anew each in its kind
For we've the gift of intelligent mind
To read, and reason, and make a choice
To praise our God with our own voice
For who can deny that he's been
When in creation his works are seen
And soon for all of eternity
We can serve him, you and me.
We thank him for his precious Son
And pray his Kingdom will soon come.

A Poem For All Of My Friends.

I'm writing a poem for all my friends,
I know how it begins but not how it ends.
You pick me up when I'm feeling blue,
And hopefully I do the same for you.
You tell me your troubles, yet listen to mine
Share each others stories when everything's fine
Together we're stronger, of that I've no doubt
You know if you need me, to give me a shout
If I'm down I may not reply, if I'm well I sure will
I love hearing your news, it gives me a thrill
Funny pictures, cartoons, and those terrible jokes
Don't detract me from you special folks
I'll help you as you are helping me
And if there's a chance we'll meet up for tea.
But for those whose home is far from mine
It's not a problem if we chat online
Our friendly rapport and support is perfection
It's great to share and keep our connection.

Best Wishes one and all.

Suppose, Suppose, Suppose.

Now suppose the sea was purple
And the sky all browns and black
Suppose you had four elbows
Or your head faced front to back.
Suppose the world was oblong
And grass was coloured blue
Or you'd grown up with three legs
Instead of the usual two.

Suppose your eyes were positioned
Upon each of your finger tips
And instead of having eyebrows there
You had teeth as well as lips.
Suppose instead of two hands
You developed three or four
And in place of your lovely ears
You had six or even more.

Suppose you needed a leg over,
Just to get into your jeans;
And your hair shot up all wavy
If you burped from eating beans.
Suppose instead of kissing lips

We tickled each other on the toes
And every time we had flatulence
It escaped loudly down our nose.

Suppose your stomach bulge was outside your body so
Everyone around you saw those digestive juices flow.
I think you'd eat more carefully
And choose with better skill,
Or is the very thought of this
Making you feel rather ill?

Suppose you couldn't get married
Until after thirty-nine
And weren't allowed to choose yourself
Just take the next in line!
Suppose they chopped you up in bits,
Once you passed age sixty-two.
Though I guess you're breathing easy now,
Supposing none of this is true!

My Brand New Driveway.

My Brand New Driveway.

I was walking past my window when did I hear a voice shout?
So I hurried out the front door to see who was standing about
But apart from a chubby chicken strutting on my lawn
I couldn't see anyone and assumed that they had gone.
As I turned to go indoors I again heard a stranger's voice
"Do you want your drive tarmac-ed I was giving you first choice."

Puzzled once more I looked around for the speaker to speak again
Then I realised that this voice was coming from the hen!
"Sorry," I gasped, "You took me by surprise, what did I hear you say?"
The chicken simply answered "I'm offering you a better driveway,
You can have it done in red or black, my squad is here in town
And we'll be glad to get started now without a penny down."

"Look, "I said, "I hope this doesn't sound as if I'm being rude,
But chickens laying tarmac, I mean, are you like any good?"
The hen she looked up at me and fixed me in her gaze
"My squad of girls are the very best as everybody says,
What's more my friend, you see me, I'm the rooster's wife
Which means I've been laying hard objects all of my married life!"

Well friends, long story short, I have gotten a brand new drive
That squad of hens worked non-stop from 7 o'clock to 5
I'm really glad I agreed for this work, and I couldn't fault the price
Because the beautiful new black tarmac laid looks oh so very nice
Best of all that chicken in charge stuck to the cost we'd agreed
Which compared to other quotes I've had this one was chickenfeed!

~~~~~~~~~~

For any non-UK readers please substitute either 'asphalt' or 'bitumen' for the word 'tarmac' to get the sense of these verses.
~~~~~~~~~~

Orbital Nellie.

There's an elephant on the moon Ma!
I saw it on the news,
The Russians put her up there,
To keep them Americans amused.

They say that you can see it,
Through binoculars or a scope,
But what about the elephant?
However will she cope?

Should she jump up and down,
Will the moon's orbit change?
Then rising tides may swamp us,
As the moon moves out of range!

Fancy spending millions
To put Nellie on the moon!
There's loads of other people
I'd prefer to have there soon.

What's that Ma, you're saying
That the Russians told a lie
And there I was believing
I'd see an elephant in the sky.

My Thoughts On Picking Up A Fallen Rose.

Ah such sweet and scented rose
Immortalised in word and song
Cherished for your beauty
But to whom do you belong?

Man has used you as a symbol
A chosen emblem in its war
Others bless you for romancing
Or for healing in their herbal lore.

Were you growing back in Eden
In man's perfect earthly home?
Surely only God designed you
A beautiful flower second to none.

In the Paradise under Jesus
We will plant yet millions more
Your coloured petals will delight our senses
As will perfume made of Rose Attar.

All praise to Jehovah our Grand Creator
For all vegetation and every tree
But most of all for the gift of roses
A splendid flower, a true majesty.

~~~~~~~~~~

Almighty God Jehovah - Revelation 4:11, Psalm 83:18 (King James Version of the Bible).
~~~~~~~~~~

I Am The Dream Merchant.

I am the dream merchant and will send you what you need
The brain has certain receptors upon which your mind will feed
For you, a simple transaction, if you want it to acquire
I'll make sure your sleep is happy and you have what you desire.
But if you snub my offers I have the power to hurt
To make your night a misery and drag you through the dirt
So carefully choose from my table, from all the dreams you find
For your sleep is very precious and it will restore your mind.

I am the dream merchant and I offer you a choice
Your dreams can be of solace and a gentle angel's voice
Or nightmares filled with terror and hateful words expressed
It's your choice as always for only you know what's best,
What is this you offer? a few shillings and no more
Friend you do insult me, you hurt me to the core
Yes I'll sell you something to occupy your brain

But you'll soon return and realise that you have to choose again.

I am the dream merchant and I have a lifetime's worth of pictures
I can give you funny, sad, or any other mixtures
As I keep on telling you, it's you that has to choose
If you want the happier dreams then money is what you use
Sell you a memory? of a happier moment in time
Certainty my darling is this what you had in mind?
A dream is but a fantasy interwoven with your life
I can add in specific people from your grandparents to your wife.

I am the dream merchant, creator of your dream
I can choose from your future, past, present, any single theme
Do you want all action, as part of your night-time's mood
Or would you prefer a woodland walk if it helps you feel so good?
I have every necessary ingredient and a trick or two besides
To make your night-time special and full of delicious rides
I'll even sprinkle in the memories of a forgotten lover or soul
So you'll wake up refreshed and happy, empowered to reach your goal.

I am the dream merchant and I am in control
Remember when you get to choose then you're on a roll
So pick and mix and then decide
I guarantee you will receive the finest nighttime ride
For my set price of course as you now know
It takes a lot of expertise to make these memories flow
Ah that's your choice, a good one fair and clean
I grant you pleasant dreams my friend for your sleep will be serene.

www.ingramcontent.com/pod-product-compliance
Lightning Source LLC
Chambersburg PA
CBHW051745130826
49812CB00033B/1005
* 9 7 8 9 3 5 7 4 4 5 4 2 9 *